Mountains

Celia Tidmarsh

HODDER
Wayland

an imprint of Hodder Children's Books

Geography First

Titles in this series
Coasts • Islands • Maps and Symbols
Mountains • Rivers • Volcanoes

© 2004 White-Thomson Publishing Ltd

Produced for Hodder Wayland by
White-Thomson Publishing Ltd
2/3 St Andrew's Place
Lewes, East Sussex
BN7 1UP

Geography consultant: John Lace, School Adviser
Editor: Katie Orchard
Picture research: Glass Onion Pictures
Designer: Chris Halls at Mind's Eye Design Ltd, Lewes
Artist: Peter Bull

Published in Great Britain in 2004 by Hodder Wayland,
an imprint of Hodder Children's Books.

The right of Celia Tidmarsh to be identified as the
author has been asserted by her in accordance with
the Copyright, Designs and Patents Act, 1988.

British Library Cataloguing in Publication Data
Tidmarsh, Celia
   Mountains. - (Geography first)
   1. Mountains - Juvenile literature
   I. Title II.Orchard, Katie
   551.4'32

ISBN 0 7502 4353 8

Printed in China

Hodder Children's Books
A division of Hodder Headline Ltd
338 Euston Road, London NW1 3BH

Cover: A mountain peak in Antarctica.
Title page: The sacred mountain of Dowa Yallane, USA.
Further information page: A hill farmer in Greece.

Acknowledgements:
The author and publisher would like to thank the following for their permission to reproduce the
following photographs: Ecoscene 10 (John Corbett),17 (Andrew Brown), 20 (Andy Binns), 25 (Andy Binns);
Hodder Wayland Picture Library contents page, chapter openers, 6, 12, 21, 31; Oxford Scientific Films cover 4
(Colin Monteath), 13 (T. C. Middleton), 14 (Colin Monteath), 19 (Mark Jones), 22 (Marty Cordano), 23
(Lon E. Lauber), 27 (Ben Osborne); Still Pictures 5 (Calvert-UNEP), 9 (Pascal Pernot), 11 (Roland Seitre),
18 (Cyril Ruoso), 24 (Roberta Parkin), 28 (Galen Rowell); WTPix 3, 26, 31.

Words in bold **like this** are explained in the glossary on page 30.

Contents

What is a mountain?

A mountain is steep-sided high land that towers more than 300 metres above the ground around it. High ground that is less than 300 metres tall is called a hill. The highest point of a mountain is called the **peak** or **summit**.

▼ *This climber is near the top of one of the highest peaks in Antarctica.*

Mountains cover one-fifth of the Earth's surface. Most mountains are found in long chains called **mountain ranges**. Every **continent** has at least one large mountain range. There are even mountain ranges under the sea.

5

▼ *These mountains in Switzerland form part of a large mountain range called the Alps.*

What makes a mountain?

The Earth's surface is a thin layer of rock called the **crust**. The crust is like a giant jigsaw puzzle, made up of smaller pieces called **plates**. These plates can move about, very slowly. If they collide with one another, the crust is pushed upwards to form a mountain range.

▼ *The Himalayas were formed when two of the Earth's plates collided.*

A volcano is a special type of mountain. Underneath the Earth's crust is a thick layer of hot, liquid rock called the **mantle**. Where the plates move apart, some of this liquid rock bursts up through the gap to form a **volcano**.

volcanoes

plates making up the Earth's crust

mountains

mantle

An ocean plate is forced under a plate from the land. The ocean plate melts and hot, liquid rock rises to the surface, forming volcanoes.

Plates move apart under the ocean and hot, liquid rock rises to form volcanic islands.

Where plates collide, rocks are squeezed together to form mountains.

Fold and block mountains

There are different types of mountains. Where two plates collide, the crust between them is squeezed upwards and folds in on itself. Mountains formed in this way are called **fold mountains**.

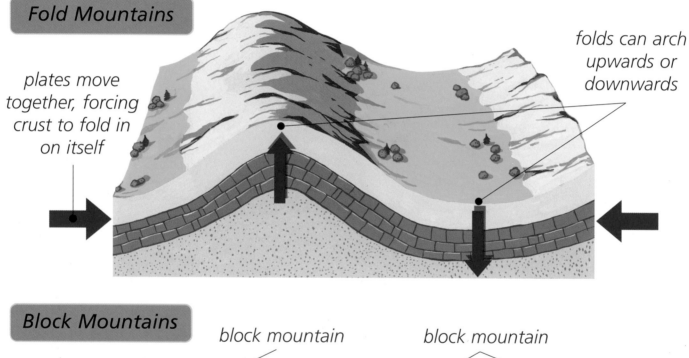

Fold Mountains

plates move together, forcing crust to fold in on itself

folds can arch upwards or downwards

Block Mountains

block mountain

block mountain

rift valley

plates move together

plates pull apart

When plates move, large cracks called **faults** appear in the crust. If the crust on either side of two faults moves together, the block of land in between is forced upwards. This forms a flat-topped mountain, called a **block mountain**.

If the crust on either side of two faults moves apart, the land in between slides downwards. This forms a flat-bottomed **valley**, called a rift valley, with block mountains on each side.

▼ *The Grand Canyon in Arizona, USA. A flat-bottomed valley runs between two block mountain formations.*

Mountains and change

Mountains are constantly changing shape. Once a mountain has been formed, the rock begins to **erode**, or wear away. The hardest rocks take the longest to erode. Erosion can happen in different ways.

All rocks have tiny cracks in them. Ice, wind, rain, and the roots of plants can get into these cracks and make them wider. Eventually pieces of rock will break off and crumble.

▼ *The rocky slope of this mountain in Pakistan has eroded. The crumbly rock is called scree.*

Rivers erode rock, too. Over time, they carve out deeper and deeper valleys through the mountains.

▲ *This river in Bhutan has worn away the rock, forming a steep-sided, V-shaped valley.*

Glaciers

Glaciers are found in many of the world's high mountain ranges. They are rather like slow-moving rivers of ice.

▼ *This is the Baltoro Glacier in the Karakoram mountains in Pakistan.*

As glaciers move they act like bulldozers, eroding V-shaped river valleys, to form deep, broad U-shaped valleys.

Thousands of years ago, in a time called the **Ice Age**, the world was much colder than it is today. There were many more glaciers found then. When these melted, the mountain landscape was revealed. The glaciers had carved out U-shaped valleys that can still be seen today.

▼ *This U-shaped valley in the mountains in Isère, France, was formed by a glacier.*

Climates

Mountains have different **climates** than low-lying areas. With no surrounding land to shelter it, the peak of a mountain is much colder than the bottom. Mountain peaks are also very windy. High peaks are covered with a blanket of snow all year round.

Lower down a mountain, the snow melts as the temperature becomes warmer.

▼ *Mountaineers in the Southern Alps of New Zealand struggle against the wind and the cold.*

Some parts of a mountain are always in shadow. They may never get sunshine and so are always cool. One side may even have more rain than another. This process is called the **rain shadow** effect.

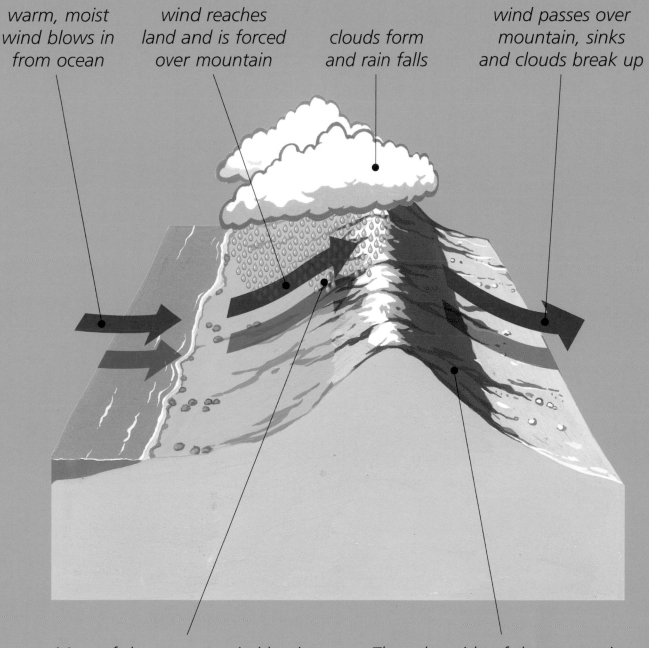

The Rain Shadow Effect

warm, moist wind blows in from ocean

wind reaches land and is forced over mountain

clouds form and rain falls

wind passes over mountain, sinks and clouds break up

Most of the water carried by the wind falls as rain on the side of the mountain nearer the ocean.

The other side of the mountain has less rain and is called the rain shadow area.

Mountain wildlife

Mountain wildlife has adapted to live in the difficult conditions. Mountain sheep and goats have sharp hooves that can grip the steep, slippery rocks. They also have thick, shaggy coats to keep them warm.

Very few animals stay on the highest slopes all the year round. Small animals, such as chipmunks and hares, live there but need to **hibernate** during the winter.

▼ *The ibex has a shaggy coat that keeps it warm in cold mountain temperatures.*

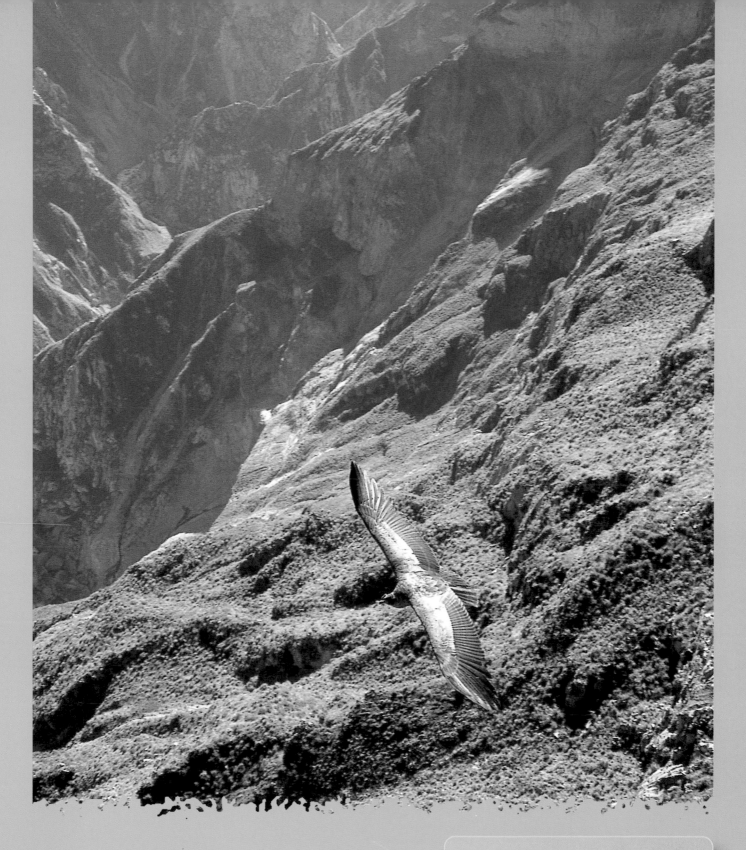

Larger animals, such as pumas, bears, wolves or gorillas, live in the forests of the lower slopes, where there is more food.

▲ *Large birds of prey such as condors glide over mountain slopes, hunting for food.*

People of the mountains

People who live in high, remote mountain areas have to adapt to the harsh environment. The steep slopes mean that there is often very little land that can be used for farming. In some places, farmers cut **terraces**, or wide steps, into the mountainside to make room for crops.

▼ *Terraces cut into this mountainside in Nepal provide enough flat space for crops to grow.*

Steep slopes are difficult to build homes on. It is also difficult to build roads and railways into the mountains. In some mountain communities, people cannot easily get from one place to another and may feel cut off.

▼ This mountain railway in Argentina provides transport to people who live in remote areas.

Natural riches

Many of the rocks that make up mountains are useful to people. Granite, limestone and marble are all rocks that are used for building. **Mines** and **quarries** have been developed in some mountains to reach these rocks.

▼ Copper mining in Arizona, USA. Copper is used for making pipes.

Mining and quarrying involve blasting large areas of rock from the mountainside with explosives. The fragile mountain environment can be badly damaged.

Forestry is another important mountain industry. Forests are often planted on the lower slopes of mountains. They provide wood for building, for making paper and for fuel.

▼ *This logging truck is being loaded with fir trees.*

Dangerous mountains

Mountains can be dangerous places. One of the biggest dangers is from **avalanches**. A loud noise may cause huge amounts of snow to slide down the mountainside. Whole villages can be buried under an avalanche. Roads may be damaged, and telephone lines swept away.

▼ *An avalanche rumbles down a mountainside in Colorado, USA.*

In the mountains the weather can change very quickly. A fine, sunny day may turn chilly suddenly as thick, low cloud moves in. The severe cold and strong winds in mountain areas can kill people if they cannot find shelter and keep warm.

▲ *Landslides of crumbling rock can damage roads or even kill people.*

Mountains under threat

Mountain environments may look solid, but they are easily damaged. Many things that humans do can harm the mountain environment.

Large numbers of walkers on a mountain may trample fragile plants and wear away the rocks. People may also cause harm by dropping litter.

▼ *These walkers in Kenya must be careful to protect the environment they have come to see.*

Many countries have opened special protected areas, or **national parks**, in the mountains. People are allowed to visit these areas, but they must not drop litter. They must also stay on signposted pathways.

▼ *In this national park in France, researchers monitor and protect mountain wildlife, such as this ibex.*

Mountain fact file

1. The highest mountain on Earth is Mauna Kea. It starts below the sea and juts up through the Pacific Ocean as an island in Hawaii. It is 10,205 metres high.

2. The world's highest mountain on dry land is Mount Everest in the Himalayas (below). It is 8,848 metres above sea level.

3. The Matterhorn, on the Swiss-Italian border, is a famous example of a sharp-peaked type of mountain, known as a 'horn'.

4. The highest mountain in Africa is Mount Kilimanjaro, in Tanzania, at 5,895 metres.

5. The Himalayas, in Asia, make up the tallest mountain range on Earth, with nearly 100 of the world's highest peaks.

6. The Andes range is the second-highest mountain range in the world. It runs the length of the continent of South America.

7. The Half Dome in Yosemite, California, USA has the most vertical mountain face in the world. It drops 670 metres.

8. The Alps stretch across parts of France, Switzerland, Italy and Austria. They were originally formed millions of years ago under the sea.

9. Australia's highest mountain is Kosciusko in the Great Dividing Range. It is 2,231 metres above sea level.

10 For many years the Rockies were a barrier between the west coast and the rest of North America. Today there are railways and roads running across them.

11 Mount Fuji, in Japan, is a volcano that is shaped just like a cone. Mount Fuji has not erupted for hundreds of years. It is Japan's national emblem.

The World's Major Mountain Ranges

Numbers on this map refer to numbers in the fact file.

Glossary

Avalanche A large mass of snow that falls down a mountainside.

Block mountain A flat-topped mountain formed when a block of land is pushed up or when surrounding blocks of land slide down.

Climate The average weather conditions of a place or area over a year.

Continent One of the large pieces of land on the Earth's surface.

Crust The thin, outer layer of the Earth.

Deciduous tree A tree that loses its leaves in autumn.

Erode Wear away.

Evergreen tree A tree that keeps its leaves all year round.

Fault A break or crack in the rocks of the crust.

Fold mountain A mountain formed when the Earth's crust is crumpled up between two plates moving towards each other.

Glacier A river of ice found high up in mountains.

Hibernate To sleep through the winter.

Ice Age A period about 18,000 years ago, when ice sheets covered much of Europe, North America and Asia.

Mantle The layer of hot liquid rock beneath the Earth's crust.

Mine A place where people have dug out rocks by tunnelling underground.

Mountain range A line or chain of mountains.

National park A special area of land that is protected from damage.

Peak The top or highest point of a mountain (also called the summit).

Plate A large section of the Earth's crust that moves about on the mantle.

Quarry A place where people dig out rocks on the surface of the Earth.

Rain shadow The side of a mountain sheltered from the rain.

Summit The top or highest point of a mountain (also called the peak).

Terrace A flat field cut like a step into the side of a mountain.

Tree-line The area on a mountain above which trees do not grow.

Valley A large trench that runs between hills and mountains.

Volcano A mountain with a hole or vent through which hot, liquid rock comes up from the mantle, through the crust and on to the Earth's surface.

Further information

Books to Read:

Geography for Fun: Mountains by Pam Robson (Watts, 2001)

Highest, Longest, Deepest by John Malam and Gary Hincks (Heinemann, 1996)

Hills and Mountains (Geography Starts Here!) by Brenda Williams (Hodder Wayland, 1997)

Mountain by Brian Knapp (Atlantic Europe Publishing, 1992)

A Mountain Hike: Green Rainbows Geography by Paul Humphrey (Evans Brothers Limited, 1994)

Our Moving Earth by Pam Robson (Watts, 2001)

Index

All the numbers in **bold** refer to photographs and illustrations as well as text.